D1526201

HISTORY OF
GYMNASTICS

KENNY ABDO

Fly!
An Imprint of Abdo Zoom
abdobooks.com

abdobooks.com

Published by Abdo Zoom, a division of ABDO, P.O. Box 398166, Minneapolis, Minnesota 55439. Copyright © 2020 by Abdo Consulting Group, Inc. International copyrights reserved in all countries. No part of this book may be reproduced in any form without written permission from the publisher. Fly!™ is a trademark and logo of Abdo Zoom.

Printed in the United States of America, North Mankato, Minnesota.
052019
092019

THIS BOOK CONTAINS
RECYCLED MATERIALS

Photo Credits: Alamy, AP Images, Granger Collection, iStock, Shutterstock
Production Contributors: Kenny Abdo, Jennie Forsberg, Grace Hansen
Design Contributors: Dorothy Toth, Neil Klinepier

Library of Congress Control Number: 2018963571

Publisher's Cataloging-in-Publication Data

Names: Abdo, Kenny, author.
Title: History of gymnastics / by Kenny Abdo.
Description: Minneapolis, Minnesota : Abdo Zoom, 2020 | Series: History of
    sports | Includes online resources and index.
Identifiers: ISBN 9781532127410 (lib. bdg.) | ISBN 9781532128394 (ebook) |
    ISBN 9781532128882 (Read-to-me ebook)
Subjects: LCSH: Gymnastics--Juvenile literature. | Sports--History--Juvenile
    Literature.
Classification: DDC 796.4409--dc23

TABLE OF CONTENTS

Gymnastics 4

Warm Up 8

Big Show 16

Glossary 22

Online Resources 23

Index 24

GYMNASTICS

In perfect form, gymnastics has stuck the landing to be one of the most exciting and impressive sports in history!

Gymnastics is broken up into many **disciplines**. Each one tests the gymnast's strength, agility, and balance. All events are scored from 0 to 10 points.

WARM UP

Gymnastics is believed to have started long ago in ancient Greece. It was supposed help the body develop. After the Romans **conquered** Greece, they made gymnastics a formal sport. It was also practiced for **warfare**.

9

10

Fredrich Ludwig Jahn was a physical education teacher in Berlin. In 1809, he invented the parallel bars, the balance beam, and the rings for his students. Jahn is known as the "father of gymnastics."

The International Gymnastics Federation (FIG) was created in 1881. It is the **governing** body of the sport. FIG sets the rules for judging gymnastic skills. This is known as the Code of Points.

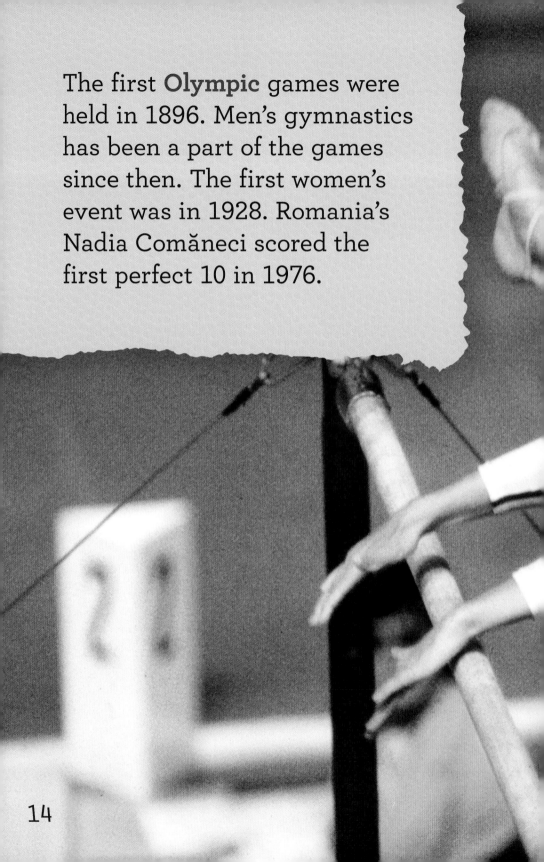

The first **Olympic** games were held in 1896. Men's gymnastics has been a part of the games since then. The first women's event was in 1928. Romania's Nadia Comăneci scored the first perfect 10 in 1976.

BIG SHOW

American Gymnast Mary Lou Retton made history at the 1984 **Olympics**. She was the first American woman to win the **all-around** gold medal. Retton's skills made her the most popular athlete in the world!

17

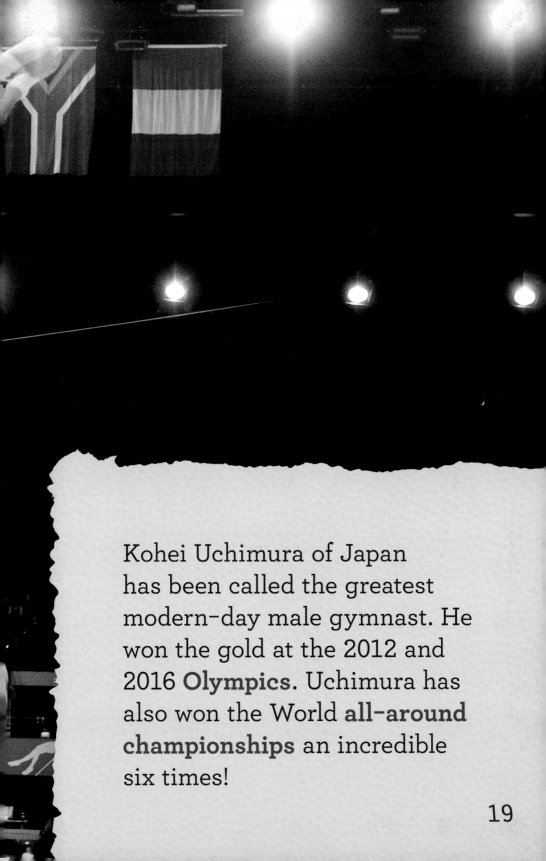

Kohei Uchimura of Japan has been called the greatest modern-day male gymnast. He won the gold at the 2012 and 2016 **Olympics**. Uchimura has also won the World **all-around championships** an incredible six times!

Simone Biles of the USA won an amazing six medals at the 2018 World Gymnastics **Championships**. She has earned 20 medals overall, the most by any female gymnast.

GLOSSARY

all-around – a gymnastics event where the scores of each exercise is totaled up to decide the winner.

championship – a game held to find a first-place winner.

conquer – to victoriously take by force.

discipline – a branch of gymnastics learned through strict practice and exercise.

govern – to enforce the rules and laws.

Olympics – the biggest sporting event in the world that is divided into summer and winter games.

warfare – fighting between differing militaries.

ONLINE RESOURCES

Booklinks
NONFICTION NETWORK
FREE! ONLINE NONFICTION RESOURCES

To learn more about gymnastics, please visit abdobooklinks.com or scan this QR code. These links are routinely monitored and updated to provide the most current information available.

INDEX

Biles, Simone 20

Comăneci, Nadia 14

Germany 11

Greece 8

International Gymnastics Federation (FIG) 12

Jahn, Fredrich Ludwig 11

Japan 19

Olympics 14, 16, 19

Retton, Mary Lou 16

Romania 14

Romans 8

rules 6, 12

Uchimura, Kohei 19

United States 16, 20

World Gymnastics Championship 19, 20